IDEAS ARMOR- INTELLECTUAL PROPERTY FOR SMES

VOLUME 2, ISSUE 3 OF BRILLOPEDIA

KRATI SANODIYA | KRISHNA TIWARI AND SEJAL

Made with ♥ on the Notion Press Platform
www.notionpress.com

Contents

Preface

"Start writing, no matter what. The water does not flow until the faucet is turned on".

• Louis L'Amour

Hundreds of students and professors are contributing their work to Brillopedia, we are here to provide ample information about Law and Contemporary issues. Our aim is to provide a platform for today's generation to express their views and ideas on law and contemporary law.

Publication

This research paper is published in volume 2, issue 3 of Brillopedia

CHAPTER ONE

With numerous SMEs working in covering and swarmed markets, the requirement for upper hands and novel selling recommendations has existed for a long time now. IPRs give that, particularly for organizations that work in the assembling or designing space. Documenting licenses, copyrights, or brand names can keep other entrepreneurs from just duplicating the thought, and it can help SMEs support their technological gain. Additionally, it can persuade SMEs that information-based developments can be similarly beneficial as raw material or labour-based ones and that scholastic exploration is vital for business achievement. It likewise shields them from exploitation – which is the greatest danger that Indian SMEs have needed to manage. In this article, we exhibit the significance and advantages of Intellectual property rights for SMEs Left at the mercy of notorious loan shark or vulnerable against more business ventures replicating a unique idea, SMEs have to deal with lost business opportunities merely because of the unawareness or the loss of expertise to file for patient, copyrights or trademarks of their products.

Further, in this article, Interception of how SMEs can protect trade secrets can help to protect the competitive space simultaneously, unleashing the untapped potential of IP, discussing the suggestive strategies for intellectual property rights for SMEs and the future benefits it beholds.

CHAPTER TWO

As a small business, it is so much easier to take pride in an innovation you came up with, to feel as if your contributions make a real difference in the world full of powerful tycoons. Having the ability to imagine simple objects and project them into authentic life creations is turned into micro-enterprises daily. However, when the large-scale industries above them exploit the creative capacity of the small businesses, it causes a considerable hindrance, and once done, there is no way to cross this stumbling block. To our answer to this obscurity, here comes our mover and shaker, i.e., intellectual property. The term Intellectual property is associated to human brain applied for creativity and invention. Countless efforts in terms of inputs of manpower, time, energy, skill, money, etc. are required to invent or create something new. IP rights are often seen as a puzzling concept. However, in a world where each country and people of interest espouses its peculiar understanding of diverse branches of law, the consistency that globally exists in intellectual property regulation is quite welcomed.

India all around world is perceived for its scholarly abilities in the fields of programming or software engineering, missile technology, Moon mission and other innovative areas. Nonetheless, India lags in age of IPR assets in terms of registered patents, industrial designs, trademarks, and so forth. In a new report by the US Chamber of Commerce, India remained at 29th place among 30 nations in IP record all around the globe. The development of any society directly depends on IPR and its strategy outline work. Lack of IPR awareness brought about the death of inventions, high risk of breach, financial misfortune and decrease of an intellectual era in the country. To such a degree, there is a critical need for dissemination of IPR information so that can boost indigenous innovations and developments in the field of research and technology. In the current cutthroat competitive environment, innovation is the backbone for each business that prompts intellectual property development. Intellectual property is not restricted to technological resorted companies and is valuable for each research and development for creating indigenous products and services. Often, SMEs are unaware of the intellectual property arrangements that bestow property and its protection, leading to more potential offers in the business industry.

Understanding the importance and the benefits showered by the IP can enhance the value of SMEs. In developing economy-driven nations like India, SMEs generate more employment opportunities than multinational firms or organizations. Intellectual property pertains to any original brand creation of human intellect viz. brands, science, art, literature, technology, or other intangible assets; they legally impart rights to that exclusive creator. Intellectual property rights are protected by the classification of the item that is to be safeguarded. These protections can take certain forms, such as copyrights or patents, depending on the actual nature, properties, and characteristics of what is to be protected.

The importance of intellectual property rights varies in countries, but it is more prominent in countries that are traded, economic driven, and developing, much like India. In the current world, the IP and its privileges have gotten more significant with internet services. As the world has gotten increasingly more subject to utilizing the web, the odds of ideas being stolen and exploited have gotten ever more elevated, and because of this, individuals or SMEs who create or find anything new need to get them licensed or protected straightaway. Misuse of innovations by different people has gotten quite possibly the most well-known violations nowadays, and the solitary victims are the SMEs. Any new startups and SMEs fail to consider their IPRs at these early stages. IP framework empowers organizations to benefit from their inventive limit and imagination, which energizes and assists stores with promoting development.

The SMEs broadly disparage its potential for providing opportunities for future benefit. IP can turn into a significant business resource if it is legally protected and demand IP-related products or services. I may create income for the SME by permitting, selling, or commercializing the IP items or services that may fundamentally improve SME's market share or raise its profit margin overall. This strategic utilization of IP can enhance the competitiveness of SMEs; they should ensure that they are ready to face challenges as these IP assets must be acquired and maintained, accounted for, monitored closely, and managed carefully to extract their total value. For this, the IP provides exclusive rights like copyright, which protects the mannerism in which the idea is shown; trademark protects the brand value, design, and logo. The Patent prohibits the use or sale of the product by another party. Depending on the type of business, the SMEs should craft their IP strategically. Although running a small-scale business involves more significant risks than large-scale organizations, the rewards are quantitative and qualitative, including broad-based prosperity and a web of symbiotic relationships.

Intellectual property rights provide several benefits for SMEs and the overall development of the nation. IP defends the competitive space; the ideas or the innovations' final product or process can be protected by a patent right that gives the business an upper hand advantage. The right to exclude others by patent protection allows ending the competition, taking the lead, and securing the market position. Interception of how SMEs can protect trade secrets also helps in protecting the competitive space. Theft or accidental revelation of trade secrets can deprive the SMEs of these advantages. Simultaneously, trademarks allow the consumers to differentiate the products and services from those of the market competitors and assurance of quality. How aesthetic the product perceives to the consumer is protected by an industrial design right is another means to distinguish it from other products. IP has untapped potential to turn these visually attractive innovations into products and services which are commercially viable. The copyright and Patent will result in a constant stream of increased income. To maintain its competitive space, an SME must be aware of the market environment; with regards to monitoring the strategies of the potential competitors, it is advised to perform IP monitoring of published patent applications, trademark registrations, and issued patents.

Another benefit anticipated is the opportunities of export business for the SMEs. The efficiency of an organization in the export market is additionally improved by intellectual property. An IP right holder may utilize these ideas to sell goods and services in foreign nations, acquire a franchise arrangement with the abroad company, or export the proprietary products. Nonetheless, organizations or individuals will attempt to duplicate the ideas or innovations for self-monetary benefits; that is why it is also essential to protect the intellectual properties so that no third party unlawfully breaches them. Thus, after analyzing the market situations, the SMEs must determine the suitable combination of Intellectual Property Rights (IPRs) to tackle these challenges. Losing shares at the initial levels can be harmful in the long run business. For almost all small and medium-sized enterprises (SMEs), marketing goods is a consequential challenge.

That is why it should establish a clear link between your products or services and the SME. This is to say, and customers should distinguish at a glance between the products of the competitors and associate them with certain aesthetic qualities.

CHAPTER THREE

The suggested strategies on intellectual property rights for SMEs are to identify SMEs' needs, the key barriers, issues, challenges, and the opportunities it holds. Sooner to build the foundation by translating and adapting the content or the publications, in general, to keep awareness and capacity-building materials on IPRs for small-medium enterprises based on their business. The main point is prioritizing the delivery of IPR services to future growth players and a continuous flow of benchmarking and feedback. An apparent IP objective can bring about successful business marketing and help position the business as an innovator in the commercial markets. With the growth in business revenues, the IP methodology can incorporate a strategy that protects the assets' unique aspects and fosters innovations to explore new geographies. This can be achieved through licensing or cojoined ventures to fabricate specified solutions that satisfy the market's unmet needs. SMEs should assess their current intellectual property to decide if it is per business goals which will assist the enterprise with recognizing better approaches to use the intellectual property.

Innovation relies on creativity. To sustain creativity in the present worldwide economy, we need a complete structure of IP rights (IPR), where pioneers can be guaranteed that their thoughts will be shielded from theft. Trailblazers need to realize that they will be made up for their creativity and hard work. Investors, as well, look for IP protection as they look for promising opportunities that will yield commercial rewards. These realities' structure a cornerstone of Prime Minister Narendra Modi's Startup India initiative. The US has a solid record of ensuring IP. Almost 33% of our labor force is situated in enterprises that are managed the cost of vigorous insurance of their developments, like aviation, data innovation, diversion, and life sciences. We accept each economy can profit by thorough and adjusted IP frameworks that secure thoughts, boost development and venture, and shield imaginative yield. India's means to fortify its own IPR environment, proclaimed in 2016 of release its first National IPR Policy, is welcome. More action is to be encouraged.

CHAPTER FOUR

In conclusion, what we know for a fact is that today, global economic leadership is present in commodities, in import substitution, or through reliance on an export-led manufacturing base. With a full fleged developed IP architecture, India can be the new pioneer of global innovations. The promise is there, the first steps have been taken, and so future seems bright. However, there is a need to fortify communication between IP workplaces, SME support institutions, business affiliations, public, regional and local governments, and other significant establishments to better recognizing the IP needs of the SMEs and the obstructions to more successful utilization of the IP system by business visionaries and SMEs. Additionally, enhancing the awareness to the SMEs about the IPRs not only patents or trade secrets but also trademarks, geographical indication, utility models, proprietary rights, new varieties of plants, non-original databases, and relevant aspects of unfair competition law among entrepreneurs and business advisers within public and private SME support institutions. As everything in the modern era is very closely connected with papers and goods under human property and is protected by statute. Without the owning party's consent, the copying, duplication, alteration, and illegal duplication of these objects will constitute a serious offense. Therefore, for SMEs, knowledge of intellectual property rights is needed and plays a significant role in the business whirlpool.